Women in INDIAN ADVERTISEMENTS

PLOTS & PERSPECTIVES

Dr. Kisholoy Roy

This book is dedicated to that one woman in my life without whom life will be very difficult to imagine. She has been an epitome of sacrifice all through her life. She has been my source of sustenance and has been someone who truly deserves to be called an immaculate homemaker.

Thanks **Ma**

Preface

In India, movies over the years have presented some extremely strong women characters on celluloid besides of course the traditional and vulnerable Ma, behen, beti etc. From Nargis in Mother India to Suchitra Sen in Aandhi, from Rekha in Khoon Bhari Maang to Meenakshi Seshadri in Damini, from Kareena Kapoor in Aitraaz to Madhuri Dixit in Gulaab Gang, from Bipasha Basu in Corporate to Tabu in Drishyam, from Alia Bhatt in Highway to Anushka Sharma in NH10 and the list can go on.

However the moot point over here is that just like movies, advertisements too have been a reflector of the contemporary society. So just as we are getting to see more women centric films today presenting women characters with steely resolve, grits and guts (movies like Pink and Mom can be cited over here), our advertisements too are frequently highlighting the new age evolved women in this country who are not afraid to take challenges, speak their mind and walk the talk. Women in Indian society today are mostly tech savvy, socially connected, emotionally stable and financially independent and they are being well represented in contemporary advertisements. Yes, there are still a plethora of advertisements that highlight women whose world revolves around domesticity and who are all caring, loving and giving for their family members. The

'Maggi' and 'Complan' mother types are still very much existent as are 'Wheel' *biwis*. But then, slowly and steadily a paradigm shift is occurring in the context and content of advertisements as far as portrayal of women in advertising in this country is concerned.

This book is classified into two major sections viz. Perspectives and Plots. While the Perspectives section majorly speaks of the conventional gender portrayals in advertisements over the years in India and abroad and mentions certain unethical practices being executed when it comes to presenting women in ads, it is the Plots section that extracts some path breaking ads from Indian advertising annals that have stood the test of time not just because of their content but the way the ads portrayed women. Such ads were found to shatter conventional wisdom about women and expectations from women in an exemplary way.

As an author of this book, I do hope and pray that readers find this book enchanting, enriching and engaging. This book can well be considered as a reference material for students pursuing MBA programs in Marketing at various B-schools in India. It can also be of help to Research Scholars pursuing doctoral research work in areas of brand communication and of course content writers engaged in content development on marketing and branding practices.

-Dr. Kisholoy Roy

Contents

PERSPECTIVES

This section mentions the various perspectives to related to advertisements and advertising. The section starts with mentioning certain basic aspects of advertising, myths surrounding advertisements, roles of advertising and then it mentions various marketing basics like Segmentation-Targeting-Positioning (or STP), Product Life Cycle (or PLC) and the 4Ps of marketing and how these serve as precursors to core advertising theory and practice. The section then goes on touch upon the issue of gender portrayal in advertisements in India and abroad. Certain unethical aspects like distasteful presentation of women in advertisements and gender stereotyping have been especially highlighted since they are directly concerned with the theme of this book. The final chapter of the section focuses on status of women in Indian society and how have they been represented in advertisements over the years. The section signs off on an optimistic note as far as depiction of women in Indian advertisements are concerned.

1.

WELCOME TO THE WORLD OF ADVERTISING

Understanding Advertising

Every product today needs strong differentiation for its long term sustenance in the market and hence they need to be promoted in different ways by the marketer. Advertising is one of the promotional tools used by marketers to promote products in various forms of mass media. Of course in today's market, advertising is often used along with other promotional tools like sales promotion, publicity, direct marketing etc. Moreover, advertising is just not restricted to print and broadcast media but we also get to find advertisements in the OOH (Out Of Home) space and advertising in the digital space. The world knows that creativity plays a big role in the development of advertisements but then it should not be mistaken that advertisements are a form of pure art; rather it is an output that should be saleable under all circumstances. An ad output is financed by a client and so the developer behind an advertisement should first and foremost cater to the interest of the client and his customer base. The creativity has to be synced with this requirement else it is not advertisement. In 1904, the famous copywriter aptly described advertisements as "salesmanship in print" since at that point of time, advertisements were strictly restricted to print media. Coming to the definition of advertising, the American Marketing Association defined it as *"any paid form of non-personal presentation and promotion of ideas, goods or services by an identified sponsor."* We thus find that the definition of advertising possess four important characteristics viz. paid form, non-personal presentation and promotion, of ideas, goods and services and finally identified sponsor. Advertisements are not a charitable activity. No corporate entity will advertise any product out of pure goodwill but in lieu of money. Thus advertisements are a paid form of promoting products. One cannot advertise oneself. As an author, I cannot advertise my own book. It has to be done by my publisher. Thus advertisements essentially are non-personal in nature. Advertisements can be developed for goods, services as well as ideas. We see advertisements of goods like biscuits, hair oil, shampoo etc and we also come across advertisements of service entities like ICICI Bank, SBI and LIC. We have also seen advertisements of ideas meant to create a better society like AIDS

Awareness, Polio Awareness, Swachh Bharat Abhiyan. In every advertisement, we do get to find the sponsor's name. The source of the advertising message viz. the sponsor is identified within the message. It is the sponsor who is paying money to the developer of an advertisement.

Myths Regarding Advertisements

Often we come across people who hold certain conceptions regarding advertisements which are wrong and can be considered as myths surrounding advertising as an activity. The first such myth is that *advertising is expenditure*. Well the fact is advertising has asset creating ability. It is an investment that helps develop brands out of generic products. It is neither wasteful expenditure nor it has short term effect. Marketers need to be patient with advertisements since benefits from this often take time to experience or to take effect. There are many amongst us who believe that advertisements are one and only solution to sell products in the market. They perceive that *advertisements alone can sell products*. First and foremost one needs to understand that marketing as an activity is based on needs and wants of consumers. Until and unless a marketer can correctly identify a need gap and develop products that genuinely caters to the requirements of consumers no amount of brilliant and saleable advertising can help matters. Advertising is to be considered as another potent tool for selling products but not the only tool to sell. There is another school of misconception about advertisements that believe that *the more you advertise, the more you sell*. Just by pumping money into advertising without any informed thought cannot guarantee extra sales. The activity of ad budgeting which we will deal later with in this course is a scientific process based on certain well scouted information from the market regarding consumption behaviour of products and media viewing habits of target audiences. Critics of advertisements often say that *advertisements are detrimental to society's well being*. Reason cited for this criticism is that advertisements promote materialism and false values. They believe that advertisements make people buy products that they do not need. However a majority of advertisements enables consumers to be informed about product features and benefits before they make purchases.

Evolution of Advertising

The earliest form of advertising was witnessed several

centuries back in fact in 3000 B C in ancient Rome. This promotional form was actually launched by the ancient Babylonians who were known to be largely materialistic. They used to write on bricks that were used to build temples and the bricks carried the name of the temple along with the king who was building it. Since the time goods were available for popular

consumption, the world saw street criers who went from street to street making public announcements of various goods like beauty remedies, fish and dairy products. Post the "Dark Ages" that followed the defeat of the Roman empire, advertising was found to regain its glory towards the end of the fifteenth century. In early 17th century, a new medium for advertising was invented in England and that was the newspaper. Newspaper advertising first appeared in America in the beginning of the 18th century. The Pennsylvania Gazette published by Benjamin Franklin in America became the largest circulating newspaper with the largest advertising volume during

this era due to which Franklin is considered the Father of American advertising. The early 19th century saw the emergence of one-man advertising agent whose job was to get businesses from advertisers, send the content of the ad to the newspaper and collect the charges. He used to keep 25% of the money obtained from the advertiser as his commission for the services rendered. The early 20th century is considered as the "Golden Age" for advertising. It was during this era that important personalities of the advertising business like F. Wayland Ayer, Albert Lasker, Claude C. Hopkins, J Walter Thompson and John E. Kennedy made their presence felt and contributed significantly to the cause of advertising. The two major approaches to advertising viz. the "soft-sell" and "hard-sell" were coined during this time. While "soft-sell" was more to do with advertisements that were presented in literary style and used subtle techniques to advertise, the "hard-sell" approach was where consumers were informed about why they should be buying a particular product. These advertisements were more straight and rational in their presentation. The 1930s witnessed Raymond Rubicam (head of famous ad agency Young & Rubicam) emerge on the advertising horizon during this time and it was also during this period that radio emerged as a popular advertising medium. The decade of 1960-1970 is considered as the decade of creative revolution in advertising business as three outstanding personalities Leo Burnett, David Ogilvy and William Bernbach spearheaded the creative pursuits in advertising products. The 1970-1980s is considered the Positioning era since the concept of positioning was introduced during this decade by Al Ries and Jack Trout in an article published

in Advertising Age journal.

In the Indian context, the Buddhists were found to rely on visual communication several

Give us this day our daily bread: with Amul Butter

utterly butterly delicious

centuries back to spread their religion. With this

objective, Emperor Ashoka was found to set up rock and pillar edicts all over the country to spread the teachings of Buddha. The first Indian newspaper was started in 1780 in Calcutta (now Kolkata). Its name was "Bengal Gazette". The first advertising agency in the country was started in 1907 in Bombay (now Mumbai). The first full fledged advertising agency in the country was luanched in 1931. Since the country gained independence, advertisements in this country have evolved with the times. Ad campaigns for brands  like Amul, Lux soap and Liril are extremely noteworthy. In fact these campaigns have achieved a cult status in the country due to their immense recall over the years. Of course there are a plethora of other advertisements and ad jingles that have caught the imagination of the mass audiences. Sylvester daCunha, Bharat Dhabolkar, Alyque Padamsee, Santosh Desai, Prasoon Joshi and Piyush Pandey are some of the notable personalities from the Indian advertising fraternity who have ensured that durable brands are created out of otherwise generic products. Some of the leading ad agencies in the country are JWT, Lowe Lintas, Chaitra Leo Burnett, Contract Advertising, Enterprise Nexus, Euro RSCG, Equus Advertising, FCB-Ulka Advertising, Mudra Communications, McCann-Erickson, Ogilvy & Mather, Rediffusion-Young & Rubicam and many more.

Fundamentals of the Advertising Business

As already mentioned advertisements are developed by advertising agencies and it is the corporate entities known as sponsors or advertisers who engage agencies to develop advertisements for their products. It is the size of a company, its overall reputation in the industry, the nature of product to be advertised and the estimated consumption potential that defines the scale of business an agency gets from a client. Once a client engages an agency to develop advertisements for a product, coordination among various departments of the agency starts so as to deliver an effective output within a deadline. Budgeting to advertise is done at the advertiser's end primarily and it is often in this context that large scale negotiations happen between client servicing team of an agency and the marketing department of the advertiser. Once an agency receives the creative brief (a document that mentions what needs to be achieved for the product through advertisement), it is passed on to the creative department of an agency to conceptualize and develop and develop a suitable output. Once the advertisement is approved by the client, the final output is placed in a medium or on various media vehicles that are considered apt by both the agency and the advertiser. There are several supplier entities of an agency without whom it is impossible to develop and place advertisements in various media. Prominent among them are typesetters, photographers, film processing specialists, printers, market researchers, film and video producers and directors. Now a days a large proportion of work concerned with ad production for the television medium are outsourced by agencies to various individual freelancers and business houses.

Careers in Advertising

There are various career options in advertising. Primarily speaking while deciding on a career in advertising one needs to be convinced that one has that creative instinct in oneself for even if a person does not get associated with the creative department of an agency one needs to approach his/her work in a creative way. An advertising agency generally recruits *Client service executives* or *Account executives* for its Client servicing department and it also hires Copywriters, *visualizers* and *graphic designers* for the creative department. The client servicing department is the interface between an advertiser and the agency as it is the client servicing executives who are supposed to represent the agency, present its portfolio of work and bag assignments for an agency. Again it is the client servicing department who are often accompanied by the personnel from the creative department when they go to showcase the draft of an ad output created by an agency. The client servicing executives thus are the main breadwinners of an agency.

Another very common and important recruitment done by agencies is that of a *Copywriter* who is often called a 'wordsmith'. It is the copywriter who is assigned the role of putting content into an advertisement. The headlines, taglines and body copy are all the brainwork of a copywriter. In a later module in this course we will have better understanding of what a copywriter does in an agency and his role in developing an advertisement.

There are people who are recruited as *Researchers/Market Researchers* in an ad agency and as *Media Planners*. The market researchers often are asked to undertake surveys regarding what approach to advertising will work in favour of a brand. They also conduct focus interviews and panel discussions after an ad is produced to understand its level of acceptability if and when it is released in the mass media. Media Planners need to study the media options for a product, the leading newspapers, radio channels, television channels, outdoor advertising entities available to reach a correct and informed decision regarding where and when to advertise a product. Buying the slots in media, scheduling the advertisements etc are principally done by the media planning and buying department of an agency. MBAs in marketing from reputed institutes of the country or people who have done courses in advertising from leading institutes of the country like MICA, Ahmedabad or FLAME, Pune are often sought after by agencies to be recruited as Client servicing executives. Even chances of being hired as Researchers or Media planning executives are also high. For the job of Copywriters, people who are fluent in English writing or the local language (for developing ads for local clients) are preferred over an MBA. Strong in literature with dollops of creativity and lateral thinking is what is required for the Creative department of an agency. For being hired as Graphic designer, suitable knowledge of DTP is required. Proficiency in Photoshop, CorelDraw and PageMaker along with knowledge of animation (certain advanced courses in this area are provided by MAAC and Arena Animation.

Advertisement Types

There are various types of advertisements. The classification is based on certain parameters like for whom an advertisement is being made, the nature of product being advertised, the nature of protagonist in an advertisement and the type of medium that hosts an advertisement. In this unit we will look at each of the classification parameters and also at the advertisement types within a category. The vastness of advertisement types will be well experienced and appreciated at the end of this unit.

Advertisement Types based on Target Audience

On the basis of target audience, there are two types of advertisements primarily viz. *B2C advertising* and *B2B advertising*. B2C stands for Business to Consumer advertising and Business to Business advertising. In the context of B2C advertising, there are four sub categories of advertising viz. *National advertising, Local advertising, End-product advertising* and *Direct response advertising.*

There are four types of advertisements that are aimed at the consumers as target audiences. National advertising is for products that have a national presence. The advertising is done at the pan-India level for the national brands. For example when we see advertisements for brands like Surf Excel, Nirma, Complan etc., they are national advertisements. Advertising done for locally manufactured products and for local retailers qualifies to be called local advertising. Adi Dhakeshwari Bastralaya is a leading garment retailer in Kolkata whose advertisements will be local advertising being done by an agency. End-product advertising is primarily directed at consumers but it is also directed at trade. Let's say an advertisement for Boeing aircraft is aimed at fliers who prefer or will prefer Boeing for certain reasons but then this aircraft has to be purchased not by consumers/fliers but the airline companies based on flier preferences. Hence here we find that end-product advertising is aimed both at consumers and at trade entities. The purpose of direct response advertising is immediate action. These advertisements are meant for products that are not supposed to pass through retail channels but are meant to be transferred directly from manufacturers/marketers to customers. Products that are sold on Home Shoppe channel on television is an example of direct response advertising.

There are four types of advertising in the context of B2B advertising viz. *Trade advertising, Industrial advertising, Professional advertising* and *Institutional advertising*. Before products are available to customers, they must be available with retailers and retailers will stock products only when they are convinced about a product's saleability. Manufacturers often use trade advertising for this purpose to promote their wares to wholesalers and retailers. Emphasis of such ads is on the profitability associated with stocking products for the wholesaler and retailer.

There are several industrial products like ball bearings, electric motor that may be the component of a consumer appliance which is being made by a company. For a company to pick up the raw materials from a manufacturer, it must be made aware and that is done through industrial advertising. In case of industrial products, advertisements do not aim to sell products but to inform about products. The actual sales happen when salespeople of a firm interact with the buying department of the purchasing firm. Advertisements that are directed to specific professionals qualify to be called as professional advertisements. When doctors are informed about new medicines or architects are informed about certain building materials, the doctors or architects take the final decision of buying on behalf of their patients or clients as the case may be. For products like medicines or building materials, the end user might not be an expert and hence it is the professional who plays a defining role in buying a product being advertised.

Institutional advertising is created to build goodwill for a company. Such advertisements mention about some positive attributes of a company and have three important goals viz. build consumer awareness and goodwill, financial relations and advocacy on a controversial issue.

Advertisement Types based on Nature of Product being Advertised

On the basis of nature of products advertised, advertisements are of three types viz. *Goods advertising, Services advertising* and *Idea advertising*. When tangible products like FMCGs and consumer durables are advertised, such form of advertising is Goods advertising. When intangible products like banking, insurance, hotels are advertised, such form of advertising is Services advertising. When advertisements are about highlighting certain thoughts, concepts and beliefs, such form of advertising is Idea advertising. Examples of the AIDS Awareness campaign and Polio campaign in India or the recently launched Swach Bharat Abhiyan by Prime Minister Narendra Modi can be cited over here.

Advertisement Types based on Nature of Protagonist in an Advertisement

Over the years, we have often observed products being introduced to us by a personality or there are advertisements where we get to see only the product in question. This is true for advertising both in print and television or internet medium. Again we have observed products being introduced to us by a celebrity at times. So in the context of nature of protagonist, there are three advertising types viz. ***Advertising featuring Celebrities***

(also called Celebrity Endorsements), ***Advertising featuring non-celebrities*** and ***Advertising featuring products only***. Examples of advertisements featuring celebrities are that of Amitabh Bachchan endorsing brands like Parker Pens, Maggi Hungroo, Complan, Dabur Glucose and many

more. We have observed that many more movie

stars and sports personalities have endorsed a range of products like FMCGs, consumer durables, electronic goods, services and even ideas. There are brands like Dove which have consciously stayed away from celebrities when it comes to advertising. They have always gone for relatively unknown faces to express their opinions about the goodness of Dove. There are many advertisements of automobiles and even personal care products where we get to find only the product.

Advertisement Types based on Type of Medium that hosts an Advertisement

Initially since the dawn of advertising, print medium had been the only source of advertisements. However with the passage of time, radio came and then came television. Since the turn of the new millennium, it was observed that OOH (Out Of Home) or Outdoor advertising gathered momentum and lots of innovation was found around us in this context. Banners, hoardings, billboards etc are various forms of Outdoor advertising. Internet was another medium in which significant innovation in advertising was observed. Thus on the basis of type of medium that hosts an advertisement, there are primarily four types of advertisements viz. *Print advertising, Broadcast advertising, Out Of Home adverti*sing and *Internet advertising.* Print advertising includes advertisements in newspapers, magazines, journals etc. Broadcast advertising includes both radio and television advertising. Internet advertising includes web banner advertising and social media advertising among various other forms.

The Roles of Advertisements

By now, we have understood that advertisements are a form of promoting products in the mass media and it is an extremely important and potent tool to make potential customers aware of a product and inform them about the features and benefits of the same. We have also learnt that advertisements do happen not just for goods but also for services and ideas. It is important to understand further that without having an acceptable product no marketer can actually hope to reap rich dividends based on great advertising. When we analyze the purpose or roles of advertisements in today's marketing landscape, we observe that the impact of advertisements, their roles and responsibilities are not just restricted to the world of marketing but they do affect the society. Advertisements do influence the way a society behaves and defines consumerism. There are four major roles of advertisements and they are – *the marketing role, the communication role, the economic role* and *the societal role*.

The Marketing Role

Not every brand is meant for everyone. There is a certain segment of people who will be interested in a product or who the marketer can consider as the potential audience/customer for a product. They are mentioned as target market in the marketing dictionary. To understand the marketing role of advertising, we take a look at the marketing concept.

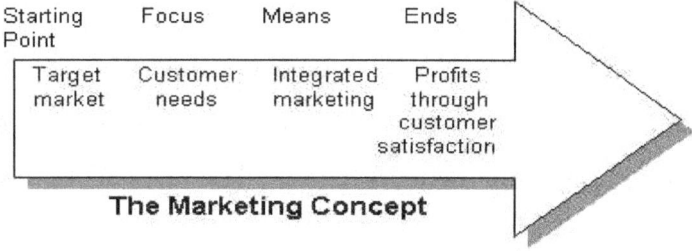

Starting Point	Focus	Means	Ends
Target market	Customer needs	Integrated marketing	Profits through customer satisfaction

The Marketing Concept

As we can see every advertisement is aimed at the target market for a product or brand. It is the needs and wants of customers that form the basis of any marketing activity for a company. Thus when advertisements are developed the focus of developing ads is to concentrate on the needs and wants of customers. The marketing concept goes for integrated marketing as means to market and communication or promotion of products is very much a part and parcel of integrated marketing. Finally the marketing role of advertising is not complete until and unless it spells revenues for the advertiser and that too through customer satisfaction. So to summarize the marketing role of advertising, it is about promoting the products to target markets that have specific needs. These set of potential customers are made aware of a brand, its features and benefits and they upon being convinced about the benefits of a product highlighted through advertisements buy the product and this contributes to profits for a company and leads to a 'win-win' scenario where both the marketer and the customer are happy with what they receive.

The Communication Role

Advertising is all about promoting products in the mass medium. It is a form of communication which is not about one to one communication but a form of communication where you can reach out to myriads of people in one go at a single point of time. Mass media like newspapers, magazines, radio, television etc ensure maximum coverage of a brand's message. Every brand in the market passes through various stages since its introduction in the market. There is a growth stage, a maturity stage and a stage which can be called a pre-decline stage where customers tend to forget a brand or new customers shy away from the brand. Reminder advertising on such occasions does help brands. Thus advertising has a communication role to play at various stages of a brand. They inform about a brand launch, keep the brand buzz alive and also ensure that people do not forget the brand.

The Economic Role

By now you as a student must have understood that there is flow of money in the economic ecosystem that is associated with the advertising activity. An agency being hired by a company against a fee, agencies placing ads in the media against a fee and finally when potential customers view an advertisement and buy the specific product, they pay money which eventually finds its way into the marketer's kitty. Hence advertising as an activity does contribute to the economic well being of a country.

The Societal Role

The final role of advertising is extremely crucial and often advertising as an activity is criticized because some lacuna is reported in this role of an advertisement. Advertisements are known to promote a consumerist society, they are supposed to create needs and wants among the audiences who view the advertisements, they are supposed to initiate certain trends in the society and bring about an overhaul in the society in the way they behave, dress, eat etc. But then advertisements are something that are targeted to kids and women and the content of a commercial is crucial enough to see to it that their sentiments are not compromised or they are not misled. Recent controversies surrounding the Amul Macho ad is an example to be cited over here. What is the product being advertised, what is the utilitarian value of the product, to what extent it serves the target market, negative connotations if any associated with the ad are various important issues that decide whether an advertisement has a socially responsible and relevant content or not.

2.

ADVERTISING IN THE MARKETING CONTEXT

Understanding the Basic Marketing Framework

Marketing and Advertising are not mutually exclusive; rather advertising has its roots in marketing and the various basic aspects of marketing. To add greater clarity to this sentence, let us understand that great advertisements are not because of the germination of some 'big idea' in the mind of the creative director/copywriter/visualizer. Rather their thoughts are guided by some analysis, some research and some information obtained through marketing efforts. To understand the pulse of target audience, you need to do market survey/market research which is a tool of marketing. Before you think of the content and approach to advertising a brand, you need to understand and analyze for whom the product is meant, how often the product will be used and what the product should mean to the target audience. In short, you are classifying a heterogeneous market into certain homogenous segments and then you decide upon a positioning statement for the product. You also need to understand the basics of integrated marketing communication and then of course suitable correlation between advertising and consumer behaviour needs to be analyzed and appreciated which will guide marketers to understand which advertisements will click and which will not and why?

The Ps of Marketing

Marketing mix is basically a tool available with the marketers that allows them to understand the basic strategies they need to develop so as to make a product acceptable to customers. McCarthy coined 4Ps of marketing as a substitute to denote the marketing mix for goods. In case of services, there are three additional Ps which constitute the marketing mix and they constitute the extended marketing mix in case of services. The 4Ps for goods are Product, Price, Place and Promotion while the three additional Ps for services are People, Process and Physical evidence. The Exhibit on the next page mentions the constituents of the 4Ps of marketing.

Marketing Mix 4 P's			
Product	**Price**	**Place**	**Promotion**
Variety	List price	Channels	Advertising
Quality	Discounts	Coverage	Personal selling
Design	Allowances	Locations	Sales promotion
Features	Payment period	Inventory	Public relations
Brand name	Credit terms	Transportation	Direct marketing
Packaging		Logistics	
Services		Assortments	

As is well understood from the exhibit and as mentioned earlier, advertising does not function in isolation. Rather the advertising strategy has to be integrated with other strategies related to Product, Price and Place and also with the other tools of promotion. Until and unless a marketer can come up with a suitable product at a reasonable price and ensures large scale and easy availability of a product, no amount of advertising or for that matter any other sort of promotion can help.

In case of services, owing to their intangibility characteristic mainly, there are three additional Ps that are of relevance. The first is the People factor or the personnel who are in charge of delivering services to customers. The way they present themselves, their product knowledge and their customer handling skills are important. Also the Process through which the service is delivered is of paramount importance. Take the case of McDonald's. Across the globe they have certain processes through which they deliver food quickly to customers and enjoy their loyalty towards the fast food retail brand. Physical evidence is another important aspect. Certain amount of tangible existence of a service adds to the satisfaction of customers. Window displays in case of retail outlets is an important physical evidence aspect.

The Promotion Mix

In this course on advertising management, we focus on the fourth P of marketing mix viz. Promotion. Advertising has its roots in marketing and the reason we say this is clear from the exhibit on this page. Advertising is a part of Promotion and Promotion is one of the components of marketing mix and that's why we say that the source of advertising is marketing. There are various forms of promotion and these together constitute the Promotion or Communication Mix. The various forms of promotion are *Advertising, Personal Selling,*

Sales Promotion, Publicity, Public Relations and *Direct Marketing*.

Advertising is a tool for promoting brands in the mass media and is largely considered a long term investment for developing brands and turning them as durable entities in the minds of the customers. Advertising is not expected to deliver quick results for brands but it takes time and lot amount of effort to build a brand. Yes 'build a brand' and that's exactly the function of advertising. Advertising contributes to brand building in conjunction with other forms of promotion that ensure revenues for marketers.

Personal selling also called direct selling is where salespeople of a company meet prospects and mention about the features and benefits of products and convinces prospects to try out a product. There can be face-to-face selling, selling over phone or through video conferencing. In short, personal selling is about one to one interaction. This form of promotion is time consuming and a marketer needs to invest on the sales person (salary and incentives of sales people).However this form of promotion facilitates clarified understanding of a brand.

Advertising builds brands but if marketers want quicker results at any point of time from a brand, it is sales promotion that they adopt. Sales promotion for brands is generally operational for a short period of time within which customers need to respond to avail a lucrative offer. They serve as incentives for the customers and the trade channel members. Sales promotions as a matter of fact are aimed at customers as well as trade channel members viz. wholesalers, stockists and retailers. The Exhibit below shows various types of sales promotions:

Consumer-Oriented	Trade-Oriented
Samples	Contests, dealer incentives
Coupons	Trade allowances
Premiums	Point-of-purchase displays
Contests/sweepstakes	Training programs
Refunds/rebates	Trade shows
Bonus packs	Cooperative advertising
Price-off deals	
Loyalty programs	
Event marketing	

You have often seen page(s) in newspapers that are captioned Advertiser's Feature where a particular corporate entity speaks about itself in detail. Many times in case of educational institutions, certain student testimonials are also to be found in them. This is what publicity is and mind it publicity too is done by agencies against a payment made by the company who is being featured. Do not be under the impression that publicity happens free as you will find many people in public domain speaking "free mein publicity ho gaya". Publicity does not come free to anyone. You pay for that. You often come across publicity of management institutes, computer training centres on the second page of newspapers or in special supplements.

Publicity is not to be confused with the next promotional tool which sounds similar and that is Public Relations. In our country the apex body in this context is the Public Relations Society of India (PRSI). Now a days each every company hire a PR agency or have an in house PR to look into various crucial issues pertaining business. The two major objectives of PR are generating good will and it also serves as a damage control measure. You must be aware of the Cadbury worm controversy or the pesticide controversy in case of soft drinks. What the companies did after that to clear the air and come back into the market with a bang holding the hands of credible celebrities like Amitabh Bachchan and Aamir Khan is public relations.

When a company sends mails, newsletters and other materials of communication directly in the name of the prospective customers, it is called direct marketing. This form of promotion allows customization and makes a prospect feel wanted by a company. Across the globe we know that Reader's Digest invests heavily in this form of promotion to enhance subscription of its magazine. The Exhibit below highlights the relative strengths of various promotional tools based on certain parameters.

Criteria	Advertising	Sales promotion	Publicity	Personal selling
Cost per audience member	Low	Low	Very low	Very high
Confined to target markets	Poor to good	Good	Moderate	Very good
Deliver a complicated message	Poor to good	Poor	Poor to good	Very good
Interchange with audiences	None	None	Low to moderate	Very good
Credibility	Low	Low	High	Moderate to high

Segmenting Markets

By now it is expected that you have understood that before advertisements are created by agencies, there needs to be certain tasks executed related to marketing that gives a clear understanding as for whom an advertisement is to be made and what should be the logical message of the advertisement. One such task is performing a S-T-P analysis for a product. This S- T- P stands for Segmentation Targeting and Positioning.

We will start off with market segmentation; the primary task of the marketer to identify which will be the most lucrative chunk of the market for a product. Market segmentation is the process of classifying a heterogeneous market into certain homogenous segments of potential buyers. This homogeneity is based on parameters like needs of buyers, behaviors of buyers etc. Segmentation is a potent tool to develop better understanding of consumers and the market associated with a particular brand. There are several levels of segmentation as mention in the exhibit given below.

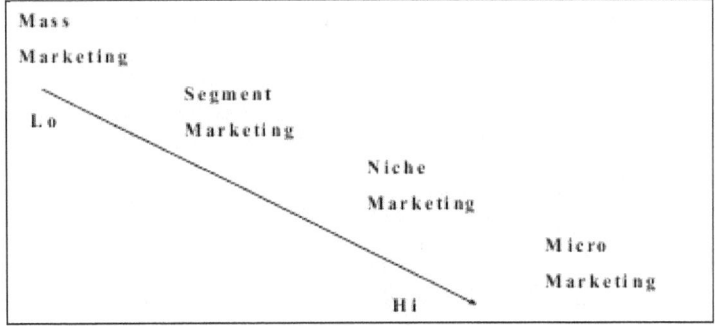

If you consider the online matrimonial market, it is micro marketing which is now in vogue and this as on date is considered the latest form of segmentation. Now let us look at the various bases of market segmentation:

- Geographic
- Demographic
- Psychographic
- Psychological
- Benefit
- Hybrid

The above are the various bases of segmentation. The first basis is Geographic segmentation where the classification is based on the assumption that people living in the same area share similar habits and wants. It is often observed by marketers that people living in urban, rural and semi-urban areas have different tastes and temperaments but then people within a particular area have similar needs and wants.

Demographic segmentation is based on characteristics like age, gender, marital status, income, occupation and education. It is the most pursued basis of segmentation pursued by marketers. In various market research surveys undertaken by companies, securing demographic details of respondents is important to understand and analyze the pulse of potential and existing buyers.

Psychographic segmentation involves a person's pattern of interests, lifestyle and values. Based on the Values and Lifestyles classification (VALS), buyers are often grouped into different categories viz. Survivors, Sustainers, Belongers, Emulators, Achievers, Experiential and Societally conscious.

Attitudes and Beliefs are the two major components of Psychological segmentation and this form of classification is often pursued by the soft drinks marketers in the country. The Youngistaan campaign of

Pepsi is an ode to the differential attitude and beliefs of today's youth.

Each individual or group of individuals seeks certain distinct benefits from the usage of a brand and often this forms the basis of classification. For a particular ready to eat packaged food product, there may be someone who is seeking convenience and again there may be someone who is seeking nutrition.

Marketers often pursue a variety of bases for classifying marketers for a particular product and this is called Hybrid segmentation.

Whatever basis of segmentation is followed, every market segment so identified needs to possess certain characteristics so that they qualify to be called an effective segment. The characteristics of an effective market segment are:

- Measurable: The identified market segment should be measurable in terms of their size, purchasing power and profiles
- Accessible: The segment needs to be suitably reached and served

- Substantial: The market segment should be large and lucrative to serve
- Differentiable: The market segment should be distinct from other market segments and should respond differently to different marketing mix elements
- Actionable: The market segment should be such that a marketer can design suitable marketing programs to serve the segment

Targeting Strategies

Once a market segment is identified by a marketer, he needs to understand as how to reach out to that segment with his marketing mix elements. There are three alternative strategies to targeting a market segment with the developed marketing mix and they are:

- Undifferentiated strategy
- Differentiated strategy
- Concentrated strategy

Undifferentiated targeting strategy is the easiest to implement since here the marketer has one set of marketing mix elements to target a particular market segment. The periphery of marketer's activity is limited since he has only one set of market segment to cater to. The marketing mix elements are aimed at the market as shown in the exhibit below.

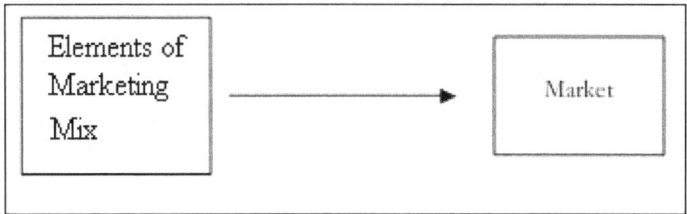

Differentiated strategy is where different sets of marketing mix elements are targeted at different groups of people taking into consideration their demographics, psychographics and other segmentation variables. In today's era a company is expected to reap greater benefits if it comes up with differentiated strategy to target markets. Differentiated strategy is shown in the exhibit below.

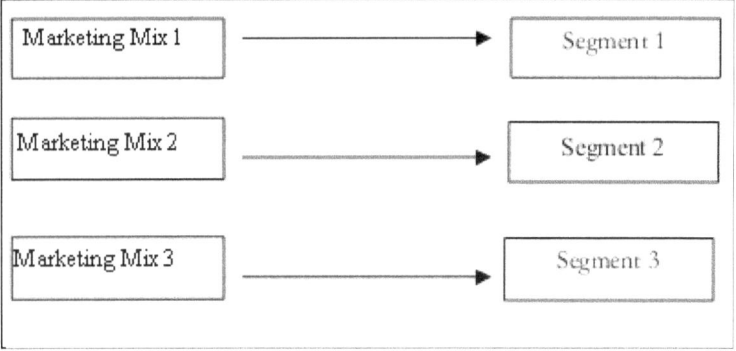

Concentrated marketing strategy is when a particular set of marketing mix elements are aimed at different market segments. Here the marketer ignores the different tastes and preferences of costumer sets that exist while targeting them with a particular strategy. This form of targeting is also called mass marketing.

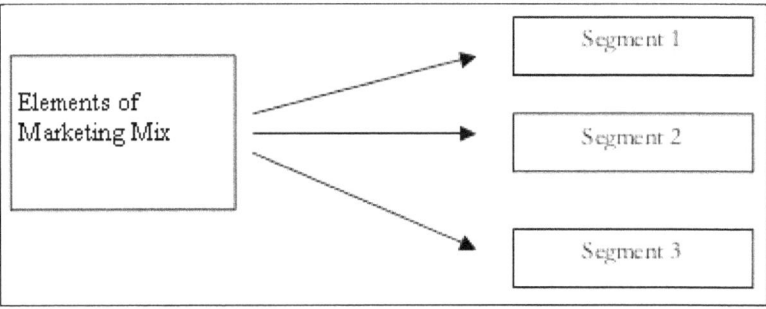

Positioning Strategies

Once a marketer classifies a heterogeneous whole market into certain homogeneous segments and then targets them applying one of the above mentioned targeting strategies, the next activity for the marketer is positioning the product. Positioning is basically a marketing strategy that aims to make a brand occupy a distinct position or space in the minds of customers vis-à-vis the competing brands. Positioning strategy acts as a fodder for developing effective advertising campaigns for brands across product categories. Brands are positioned in seven different ways:

- Using product characteristics or customer benefits
- Using the price-quality approach
- Based on the use of product approach
- Using the product-user approach
- Using the product class approach
- Using the cultural symbol approach
- Using the competitor approach

Many of us do remember the Vicks ads or the Vicks Action 500 ads (that talked of "kuch lete kyon nahi"). It was a classic example of positioning a brand using the use based or rather the time of use based approach. The Incredible India campaigns are positioned based on the cultural symbol approach. The price-quality approach is one of the most pursued methods of positioning across product categories where a comparative analysis of brands is done on the basis of price vis-à-vis quality. The competitor approach is another pursued approach my marketers. For rent a car services in the US market in 1960s, it was found that Avis was ranked second behind Hertz. Now when Avis positioned itself to attract customers it said why people should choose them..it is because they are No. 2 and they try harder. It was this trying harder proposition that stayed on with the brand for the next 50 years. Such statements coined by companies across the globe are called positioning statements. A positioning statement is basically a statement of differentiation and it basically an expression of what sets a brand apart from the competition.

In the context of positioning, we need to discuss over here another marketing term called USP or the Unique Selling Proposition. While positioning always exist in a market and every brand has a positioning statement, it is not possible for each and every brand to have a USP since it has to be something which is not physically present in the market and no something that has been created using words and emotions in the advertisements. Rosser Reeves coined the term USP in 1940. A USP thus has to be something which the competition is not offering and secondly it should be strong enough to appeal to a large cross section of potential buyers.

Another marketing term to be discussed over here is perceptual territory. Brands are positioned vis-à-vis competing brands and every marketer aims at clinching the most favourable position in the minds of customers so that the brand enjoys top of mind recall and loyalty. The minds of customers are also referred to as perceptual territory which gives a clear picture how is a brand perceived vis-à-vis competition. Graphical representations of the consumer mental landscape are called perceptual territory or perceptual map or mental map. The exhibit below shows one such sample representation.

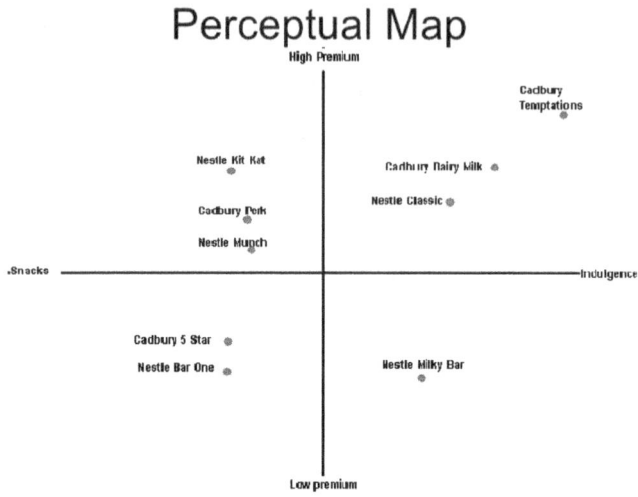

Perceptual Map

High Premium

Cadbury Temptations

Nestle Kit Kat

Cadbury Dairy Milk

Nestle Classic

Cadbury Perk

Nestle Munch

Snacks — Indulgence

Cadbury 5 Star

Nestle Bar One

Nestle Milky Bar

Low premium

Introducing Product Life Cycle

Every product in the market goes through certain phases since its introduction in the market and every marketer needs to keep tweaking its strategies accordingly so that the product is successfully managed throughout its life cycle. There are certain basic goals of managing product life cycle viz. reducing time to market, improving product quality, identifying potential sales opportunities and reducing environmental impacts towards the declining phase of a product. The Product Life Cycle (PLC) comprises four stages through which a product passes viz. Introduction, Growth, Maturity and Decline as shown in the exhibit below.

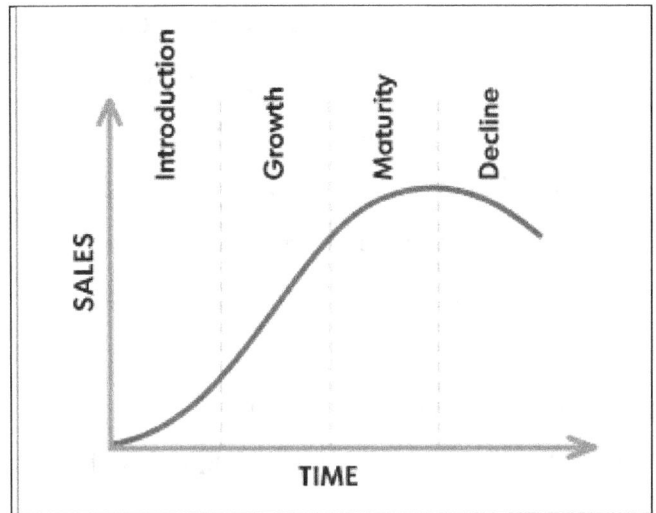

As can be seen from the exhibit, the PLC curve is a bell shaped curve. The 'Time' element is plotted on the X axis while the 'Sales' element is plotted on the Y axis.

Stages of Product Life Cycle

As mentioned in the previous section, there are four stages in the Product Life Cycle. In the Introduction stage, a company tries to build product awareness and develop suitable demand for the product in the market. During this stage, branding of the product and quality level of the product are established. In case of competitive market scenario, penetration pricing strategy is adopted generally by companies. But then, if competition is insignificant, companies have been found to adopt market skimming pricing strategy also where companies are found to fix a higher rate of products in order to garner as much revenues as possible before competition sets in. Promotion of the products during this stage is mainly aimed at those sets of customers who are willing to experiment new products.

In the Growth stage of the Product Life Cycle, a company tries to build preference for the brand and increase its market share. Quality of the product is maintained and certain additional product features might be incorporated. Pricing strategy adopted in the Introduction stage is often maintained in this phase since significant product demand exists. Certain channels of distribution for the product may be added. The promotion of the product is now aimed at a broader audience.

In the Maturity stage of the Product Life Cycle, it is observed that strong growth in sales of the product starts diminishing as newer competition arises during this phase. Product features are added during this phase to differentiate the product from competition. Pricing of the product may be lower because of new competition. Distribution of the product may be intensified. The promotion of the product is targeted at product differentiation.

The Decline stage of the Product Life Cycle signifies decline in sales of the product. A firm may have several options to try out at this stage. It can maintain the product or can rejuvenate it by adding new features or adding newer meanings to the product. Reducing prices of the product or selling the product to any other marketer or taking the product off from the market totally are some of the other options. The exhibit below highlights the corresponding characteristics of various identifying parameters at various stages of the Product Life Cycle.

	Stages			
Identifying features	Introduction	Growth	Maturity	Decline
Sales	Low	High	High	Low
Investment cost	Very high	High (lower than intro stage)	Low	Low
Competition	Low or no competition	High	Very high	Very High
Advertising	Very high	High	High	Low
Profit	Low	High	High	Low

PLC and Advertising Types

Based on the various stages of the product life cycle, there are different forms or types of advertising viz. Pioneering, Competitive & Comparative and Reminder. Refer to the exhibit below.

Pioneering advertising is designed to generate primary demand for a product and it is often used to a large extent during the Introduction stage of the product life cycle. Since this type of advertising provides in-depth information on the benefits of using a product, it is often called Informative advertising. Advertisements of products during the introductory stage require information to be disseminated to the public for the surge in its demand to happen later on.

Competitive and Comparative advertising is generally observed during the Growth stage of the product life cycle. The companies provide such information about their products that are not being offered by competing brands in that product category. Those brands may have similar attributes but it is this advertiser who gives an impression to the market that it is only his product that has these attributes. This often happens in case of electronic goods. In Comparative advertising, two or more brands are compared on various attributes to amplify their existence. This is often observed in case of financial service products. Both these forms of advertising have been largely noticed in the Growth phase.

Since the Maturity stage and later during the Decline stage of product life cycle, demand of the product starts diminishing and the product starts loosing its relevance in the market. Reminder advertising is an attempt by advertisers to make people realize about the product's existence over the years, the unique and sustainable attributes of its and offering a strong reason why should people continue with the brand in future.

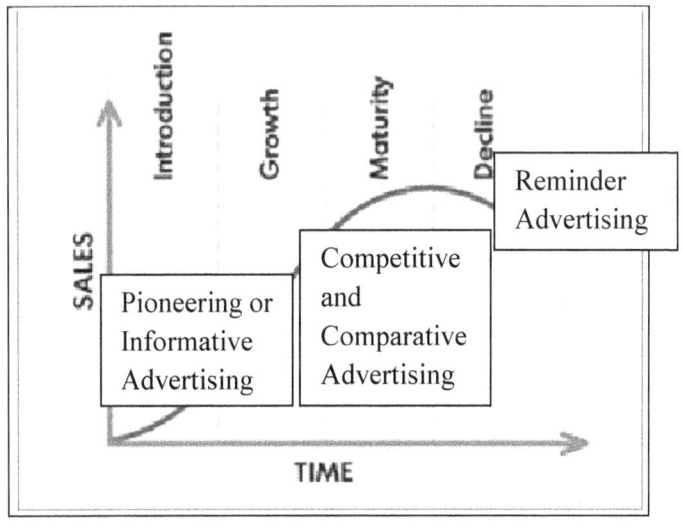

The Communication Process

Any communication is said to be effective only when both the sender and receiver of a message are happy and satisfied with each other's efforts and with the overall outcome of the communication. In the context of marketing communication, it is observed that there is a sender who is the advertiser and who has a message to communicate. This message is sent via some medium or media for which the message needs some kind of formatting to suit the media format and the recipients of that format. This formatting is called encoding which is done by the advertiser. Once the message passes through the media, for the message to be understood, the receiver which happens to be the target audiences decode or decipher the message content for their suitable understanding. They respond to this message by

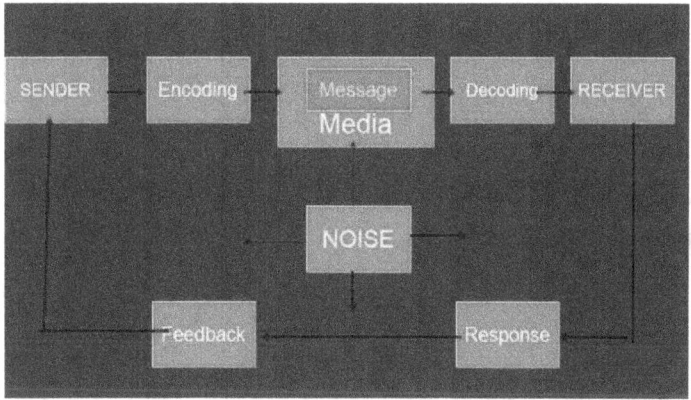

purchasing/not purchasing a product which actually turns out to be a feedback for the advertiser as to how well his communication has performed. But then many times, it so happens that the advertiser is unable to encode the message properly. The communication is misunderstood or some unwelcome meanings are gathered by the recipient upon interacting with the communication and then this communication looses its purpose and it turns into noise which is nothing but wastage of time and efforts on the part of the advertiser.

There are also certain other reasons why a communication initiated by the advertiser does not reach the target audience or it does not perform the intended function with the target audience. Three such reasons are *selective attention, selective distortion* and *selective retention*.

It is often observed that a target audience is interested in only particular kind of products or in a particular brand and actively listens to responds to communication in that context only. In other words communication for all other product categories and brands will turn into noise for that person. This is called *selective attention*.

People often want to understand a message delivered by the advertiser the way they want to and because of this, messages often end up as noise. There is a distortion of intended message delivered by the advertiser and this is called *selective distortion*.

People like to remember certain events, communication which they like and which they feel like recalling again and again and this is *selective retention* while they rest they want to forget. Think about ad campaigns of Liril soap, Youngistaan commercials of Pepsi and many such campaigns. It is the selective retention factor that has worked in favour of these brands.

3.

GENDER AND ADVERTISING

The Concept of Gender

The Oxford English dictionary defines the word gender as either of the two sexes (male and female), especially when considered with reference to social and cultural differences rather than biological ones. The word gender is also used more broadly to denote range of identities that do not correspond to established ideas of male and female. It is a socially constructed identity that rests on a binary dyad and comprises of both men and women. The word gender talks of not only the socially constructed differences between men and women, but also the stereotypes of masculinity and femininity. Masculinity is defined as the state of 'being a man' while femininity is not necessarily seen as the state of 'being a woman'; but it is perceived more as a stereotype of a woman's role from the past.

Erving Goffman in his book *Gender Advertisements* mentions that gendered behaviour, as well the concepts of masculinity and femininity, are scripts which are dictated by the environment that consciously and unconsciously are learned and performed by persons in order to play their appropriate roles in society. It is an established norm across many nations that within a family, while men perform the role of bread earners, women function as homemakers. The differences between men and women generate common gender role stereotypes. Many behavioural scientists opine that women are to be considered as nature and men as culture. Over the years, men have been found to control the nature through culture and thus considered superior to women.

The Conventional Gender Roles

For centuries, men are known to be financial providers, career-focused and independent, whereas women is the gender having domestic responsibility linked in to her role as loving wife, caring mother and low-positioned worker, undertaking the bulk of house hold work. In recent times, feminist movements have created significant impact in changing the roles and statuses of women in the society. Such movements have aimed to eradicate traditional expectations around women and the discriminations made against them right from the time when they are born. Today's society exhibits several instances of families based on a partnership rather than on patriarchy attitude.

Despite certain positive changes being reported in the 21st Century, there are many men who still like to fit in the role of masculinity, but for modern women, being and fitting into the role of feminity, has not been a very important need. The concept of feminity has been redefined as on date as it is no more a word to depict vulnerability and meek surrender to masculine demands and expectations; rather it is about being confident and assertive and do what one prioritizes in life. However in this context there are many who observe that it is very difficult for women to manifest, their autonomous individuality and their feminine destiny at the same time. Cultural and historical context have a significant role to play over here. While Western women strive more to establish their individual identity, the Asian women find solace by improving the economy of their family and their status within the family. In the present day world, although men and women are leading highly complex lives with multiple societal roles to fulfil, still the primary and prevalent societal expectation from men is to be bread earners and women to be home makers.

Modern societies in most developing countries can safely be considered as progressive but then the conventional thinking regarding roles of men and women still exist. However with social and economical development, the gap is sure to narrow down. Like any popular form of entertainment or infotainment, advertisements do influence society and societal thinking process. Advertisements often are a mirror of the society and along with promoting brands, advertisements often have the capability to send a strong message to the society in context aspects like gender roles. However advertisers over the years have largely been found to use traditional gender stereotypes in their commercials with an assumption that they are well known and will be accepted by everyone without much fuss.

Before we look at the kind of role that gender plays in the advertising stratosphere, let us discuss some of the ethical aspects of advertising. There will be at least two areas among the ethical issues related to advertising that will be leading us to the topic of the role of gender in advertising.

Advertising and the Ethical Aspects

Wikipedia describes Ethics as a branch of philosophy that includes systematizing, defending and recommending concepts of right or wrong conduct. Just like any business activity, advertising too has constantly been faced with ethical issues and challenges over the years. Ethical issues must be considered in all integrated marketing communication decisions as at the end of the day, any advertising communication is meant for audiences who will eventually convert into buyers/consumers post seeing an ad. It is critical thus to communicate with accuracy and transparency about goods and services being advertised.

Ethics in advertising involves a set of well defined principles that govern the way communication between the buyer and seller take place. One can safely define an ethical advertisement as a communication which does not make false claims and is within the limits of decency. Another aspect to be kept in mind is that ethics in advertising is directly related to the purpose of an advertisement and the nature of advertisement. The content of any advertisement should be in tune with the product nature. Needless innuendoes in advertisements are often not considered ethical. A classic example from Indian advertising to be cited over here is the ad for Tuff Shoes couple of decades back when a nude Milind Soman and Madhu Sapre donned Tuff Shoes and shared a python between them. The ad became not just an all time controversial advertisement in Indian advertising history but was largely considered unethical due to lack of sync between the nature of product and the advertising content and for misleading the perceptions and conclusions of target audiences for the brand. Advertising is one activity where if anything unethical is spotted  it becomes quickly visible which can eventually lead to damaging the reputation of a company.

Although various regulatory bodies are present in our country as well as in other countries, but then the best form of regulation is self regulation which can be followed by advertisers by committing to the following:

- Designing self regulatory codes which will include ethical norms, truth, decency and legal points
- Tracking advertising activities and removing those advertisements which do not conform to the codes set
- Informing consumers about the self regulatory codes of the company
- Sincerely attending to customer complaints regarding the product advertisements
- Maintaining transparency across the company and systems involved

Because of the absence of self regulation, the role of advertising in society is often found to be controversial. Advertisers are often criticized for using tools and techniques that are deceptive, exploitative, controversial, offensive and often propagate stereotyping. Let's take a look at the various significant criticisms of advertisements:

Advertisements Make Fake Claims and are Deceptive

Although advertisements are supposed to stay transparent while promoting brands, ironically one of the major complaints against advertisements is that they are deceptive in the way they project brands. Often we come across advertisements that mention superlatives like The Best, The Most, The Strongest or even The No 1 when reality is far from what is being mentioned. Although many in advertising circles call it legal and further say that this is puffery which involves the exaggerated or impossible claims, but then there is a subtle difference between being legal and being deceptive. Use of emotional appeals is another area of concern as this appeal is often used by advertisers to wrongfully woo potential consumers towards buying and using a brand. Advertisers of products related to beauty and prestige often go for such tactics. Advertisements of beauty products often make false and misleading claims but they weave such convincing plots while telling the brand story that people often get wooed by the brand claims. In India, Fair & Lovely is one beauty product that has often got into controversy due to this and many other reasons. Although while conceiving and executing creative strategies for brand communication, it is often difficult to be clear about the ethical angle but then as mentioned earlier, ethical norms within a company need to be well spelt and transpired so that each and every individual knows the 'limits' and works accordingly.

Advertisers Promote Controversial Products

Certain products like tobacco, alcoholic beverages, gambling and lotteries are considered taboo by many within a healthy society and hence there is an ethical aspect that comes to the forefront when advertisers try  promoting such products in the media. In India and in many other countries too, advertising products like tobacco and alcoholic beverages is banned as per the seventh rule of the Cable Television Network rules, 1999. The rule states that advertisements that promote directly or indirectly the sale or consumption of cigarettes, tobacco products, wine, alcohol, liquor or other intoxicants, infant milk substitution, feeding bottle or infant food are not permitted. But then advertisers have found out clever ways of reaching out to audiences through surrogate advertising route. Basically speaking, surrogate advertising is about promoting banned products like cigarettes and alcohol in the guise of another product like CDs and cassettes, packaged drinking water, soda etc. keeping  the spirit of the original brand alive and that is what is a matter of concern. Brands  like Kingfisher, Bagpiper, Royal Stag and Wills Filter cigarettes have all resorted to this form of advertising over the years in India.

Comparative Advertisements and Compromising on Ethics

Comparative advertisements are those where an advertiser makes a comparison between the firm's brand and the competitor's brand by showing the competitor's product as a weaker one. Often the brand name of competitor is invisible but then the colour and other brand elements of the competitor product give clear indication of the brand being compared with. However in the quest of this comparison and highlighting oneself as the superior one, companies often indulge in unfair means which is considered highly unethical. Making fun of the advertising context of competitors product has been noticed vividly in case of

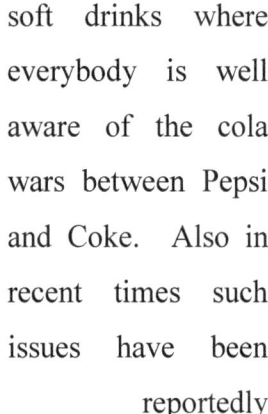

soft drinks where everybody is well aware of the cola wars between Pepsi and Coke. Also in recent times such issues have been reportedly happening in women's personal care segment (hair removal alternatives) where there is a tussle between Gillette's shaving products and Veet hair removal cream. As per the guidelines set up by the American Association of Advertising Agency, it is not allowed to use the competitor's product, service, brand name and logo as point of references in comparative advertising. Issues with comparative advertising have been reported in the detergent cake category (Nirma and Rin) and also in health drinks category (Horlicks and Complan).

Advertisements are often distasteful

There are certain advertisements which have over the years come to the limelight for all the wrong reasons. They have been criticized for being vulgar, distasteful, offensive and irritating. There are certain products like condoms

and personal hygiene products that often adopt the same colour and flavour of communication which is irritating to audiences. Internationally, advertisements for brands like United Colors of Benetton have been criticized for showing disrespect to various races and religions of the world. Advertisements for lifestyle brands like Dolce & Gabbana Abercrombie & Fitch have been equally distasteful as they have often indulged in commoditization of women and portraying them as cheap objects of pleasure by men.

One of the most common reasons for audiences to feel offended about advertisements is the unwarranted use of sex and sensuousness and unacceptable body language of models in advertisements across product categories. An example that can be recalled in this context is an advertisement for Bisleri packaged drinking water many

 years back where a semi nude woman is seen lying on a beach with the tagline 'Play Safe'. The visual definitely is not in sync with the product category in question and moreover the tagline along with the visual suggests something uncalled for. Irritating benefits being

aired about men's undergarments is another aspect to be mentioned. Also type of appeal used for such advertisements is highly questionable at times. The tagline – "Yeh to bada Toing hai" for Amul Macho was disgusting to say the least. The advertisement was severely criticized in the media for being vulgar as it showed a woman openly washing the Amul  Macho brief of her husband conjuring images of conjugal bliss with her husband. Liberal doses of sexual appeal and portraying women as objects of pleasure, sweet nothings and in compromising positions demean the dignity of women which lead many to question the ethics of advertisers across nations.

Advertisements propagate stereotyping

Another extremely critical issue concerned with ethics in advertising is that advertisements propagate gender stereotyping. Various research studies conducted over the years show the constant occurrence of gender stereotyping in advertisements, with a little variation over the years. The studies highlighted that over the years women are portrayed as either preoccupied with their household chores or are portrayed as decorative pieces to attract eyeballs towards an advertised brand or as sex commodities. Who can forget the introduction of liberal doses of sexual elements while advertising men's personal care brand, Axe. Here we find women being presented to promote a brand  which has nothing to do with women as far as using that brand is concerned. The ads clearly suggest women as cheap entities surrendering to the so called 'Axe Effect!" There are instances where even body parts of women are objectified to sell products a range of products.

Men on the other hand have over the years been portrayed as constructive, adventurous, and powerful. Although our society has been witnessing a move towards gender equality, advertisements unfortunately have been unable to join the bandwagon.

Over here, i will be interested in presenting an old time international advertisement of a cigarette brand called Nico Time cigarettes. You will agree that this advertisement not just promotes a controversial product or rather a health damaging product blatantly but its also unethical since it attempts at fostering the idea  of smoking in pregnant women which is definitely detrimental to their health and the foetus. It further attempts at gender stereotyping by using the word 'crave'; something which is so commonly used to describe feminine tendencies and attitudes.

Ideally advertisements should be a societal reflector but then that role has sadly not been accomplished as they have often failed to depict accomplishment of women and the rapid strides that women have taken across various verticals in the society. Research studies have proven beyond doubt that focus of advertisements has been on men, their concerns, their actions, their accomplishments, their woes while there has been step motherly treatment being meted out to women. Even issues and problems of women have been discussed in hushed voices in advertisements as if discussing such issues is a taboo; as if women are marginalized creatures in the society.

Gender Depiction in Advertisements

Across the globe and over the years, advertisements have painted gender in distinct and predictable stereotypes. Gender depictions in advertising reflect "fundamental features of the social structure," viz. values, beliefs and norms.

Research studies on gender role depictions in television advertisements conclude that women appeared more often as housewives in television advertisements. Studies have also indicated that women have mostly been depicted as sex commodities, physically beautiful and subordinate in advertisements targeted at television audiences. Traditional representation of women in advertisements has been as a housewife, mother, domestic help, unskilled or semi skilled worker etc who have been found to either solve domestic nitty gritties or carry out jobs as per instructions of superiors. In short, such activities that require less of mental effort and intellect leaving women to be considered almost a worthless gender. Women have been found to appear in commercials for cosmetics, kitchen and bathroom products which clearly indicate that either they are considered as beautiful creatures to lure men or are home bound. Women are mostly shown in home setting to convey the message that the women's place is at home. When it comes to advertisements of consumer products, men are often depicted in positions of command, power etc. where as women are hardly portrayed presented in such positions. , and are rather positioned as an object of stare. To summarize the statements made above, it can be safely said that gender representation in advertisements highlights the ideology of the active and public male and the passive, dependent, domestic female.

The trends in gender representation in television commercials show that unequal gender representation is still present in television commercials. Advertisers find it easy to communicate to a target audience with existing beliefs, and thus sell their products rather than going for application of multiple, realistic values and beliefs. While the perennial aspect of female representation in advertisements is appearance, which is more often in passive and submissive pose, the defining feature of male representation is action or activity in advertisements.

When it comes to celebrity endorsements, a form of differentiated brand promotion strategy in the context of advertisements, similar aspects have been reported. While male celebrities are generally associated with the visual plus verbal presentation style and functional product benefits, female celebrities are associated more with the visual presentation style and with psycho-social product benefits.

There are certain studies that explore that though women are portrayed as young in majority of television commercials and rarely in professional roles, their decorative roles for men's product are declining and neutral role portrayal of women is increasing.

Women are also being increasingly shown as acting independently of men in choosing recreational activities and as product representatives in advertisements. They are to be found voicing their thoughts on children education and playing a defining role in families on various matters.

Instead of coming up with more advertisements that highlight intellect and grit of women, most advertisements have taken pride and pleasure in commoditization of women and their body parts excessively and unnecessarily. As mentioned earlier in this chapter, the ethical issues of advertisements being distasteful and creating gender stereotypes are something that are closely associated with gender depiction in advertisements across countries. These two aspects can well be treated as precursors to the next chapter on Indian women and their portrayal in advertisements over the years.

4.

WOMEN IN INDIAN ADVERTISEMENTS

Women in Advertisements across Nations

It is interesting to study gender role portrayals in advertisements in various countries of the world. In Asian countries like Singapore and Malaysia, the depiction of men and women in advertising have been influenced by several factors like the culture of the country and the traits of the target audience. As is the case with most Indian advertisements we know of, advertisements on Malaysian television depicts men in independent and macho avatars while women are portrayed as young housewives, whose main responsibility is to take care of the house and children. Women are mostly found promoting personal and beauty care products. However when it comes to television advertisements in Singapore, gender stereotypes are less stringent. Women are shown as employed individuals in white-collar jobs and in service industry.

Overall various research studies conducted round the globe have concluded that there has been very less of change as such when it comes to overall content and nature of television advertisements round the globe since the 1970s. Of course gender stereotyping is more prevalent in Asian countries rather than the western world. While this phenomenon is seeing a rapid decline in countries like the US and UK and many other European countries, no such well marked change can be found in television advertisements of Asian countries. A study of advertisements of various Middle eastern countries show women promoting brands wearing long dresses covering their bodies and further they are to be found in advertisements only when the product in question is something related to women like cosmetics and food products or household appliances.

Although its a fact that gender stereotyping is on the decline when it comes to the western countries, it is yet to be considered insignificant since studies find that women are underrepresented as primary characters during most prime time commercials except for health and beauty products.

The element of sexuality is significantly present in ads of many countries but then degree and frequency of its depiction differs as studies reveal that while Chinese advertisements show much lower degrees of sexuality, Thai and French advertisements show the highest levels of sexuality. Advertisements of another South-east Asian country viz. South Korea also show women as dependent individuals nurturing children and taking acre of home but then most advertisements present women as the central character in an ad. Thus stereotyping exists over there although their society has progressed a lot over the years.

Another important aspect to note is that while various fashion magazine ads in the U.S. exhibit traditional gender roles and portray more non-working women and women as a attractive objects; the French advertisements depict contemporary gender roles and show more men being with family.

Representation of gender role in advertisements across countries mainly depends on the cultural values and gender norms of a country. Portrayal of men and women in Indian Television advertisements are more in sync with other Asian countries than the countries in the West. Women are being presented more in traditional roles rather than the roles women are increasingly taking up in real contemporary world. As discussed earlier in this section, it is about dominant norms prevailing in the society and the overall cultural mindset of people that often dictates gender portrayals in advertisements of a country.

Women in Indian Society

Actual progress of a society, community or a country can only happen when its women folk prosper, advances and assume defining roles in the society. Women bring with themselves the power of emotional connect, dedication etc which translates into greater common good and hence it is observed that what a man can do with a task, if a woman takes charge of it with the right intention, she surpasses her male counterpart. Increase of positive female influence in various facets of the society would affect the advancement of society in a definite way. More liberal are the women in a society and more liberal are their thoughts, there will be more progress. Societies that offer its women a claustrophobic environment are seldom found to make advances. The best way thus to evaluate the status of women in any group is to examine different role played by the women and the trend and pattern of their performance

The dawn of Indian history has evidence of women being worshiped as incarnation of goddesses. Manu, one of the great lawgiver of ancient India observed that where women are honoured there resides God. It comes as no surprise thus that women constituted the root of Indian civilization. The Ramayana and Mahabharata depicts some extremely strong women characters in Sita and Draupadi who were strong willed, who were honoured and it was for the safeguard of their dignity that fierce battles were fought.

The status of Indian woman has witnessed many ups and downs over the years. The way the status of women in Indian society has fluctuated with eras is an exciting study where one gets to find women having equivalent status in ancient times through the setback of the medieval period, to the promotion of equal rights by many social reformers. Although there is a belief that from 19th century onward the status of women has improved, but according to many, modern development paradigm has marginalized women and their status and there has been an erosion in their status as compared to the pre-colonial times. It is actually a matter of great shame for a country like India whose ancient civilization held women in such great esteem while its modern day civilization dishes out so much of discrimination which is gender based. Women in modern India face discrimination when it comes to education, choice of profession, their conduct at public places, what they wear and many more. They are ogled at by men rampantly, eve teased, molested and raped. At many places in modern India raping a woman has become a favourite pastime for the men folk. The poor legal infrastructure, the societal pressures make it difficult for most women to report cases of crime against them and to seek justice for themselves.

The patriarchal societal structure in India gives a damn as far as a woman's individuality is concerned. She is expected to be known as someone's daughter, wife and mother in a family and not because of herself and her own skill sets. According to the first literary treatise, i.e. Rig Veda, though early Vedic families were patriarchal in nature, women were never denied their rights. They had some control on the affairs of their household and enjoyed equal status with their male counterparts.

However in the Post-Vedic age, a gradual decline in the status and position of women in India was reported due to the prevailing customs and traditions of the society like child marriage, sati-pratha, widow harassment, mainly the patriarchal joint-family system, rules of ownership of the properties, etc. Women were found to loose their identity in society. The society started restricting activities of women and the men in the society started considering women either as temptations or as hurdles in their quest for higher development. As per Manu, the progenitor of Hindu race, girls are supposed to be in the custody of their father during their childhood, under the custody of their husbands when married and under the custody of their sons as widows and she will be someone who will never demand independence. The Pardah system has been the brainchild of the patriarchal mentality to curb women's power to communicate with the external world and this system is not something related to only the Muslim religion but even in elite Hindu families being described by literary doyens in this country like Rabindranath Tagore, Sarat Chandra Chattopadhyay and Bankim

Chandra Chattopadhay, it is a documented fact that women in such families were to stay indoors and it was considered inappropriate and against societal norms if a woman was found to speak to any outsider especially if that outsider is a male.

The British rule in India offered the scope to many women in this country to join the freedom movement under the leadership of various national and regional freedom fighters. Education institutions for women were set up in major cities. With the country gaining freedom in 1947 what followed were numerous provisions in our constitution that heralded a new era of equality for Indian women. With the passage of time, women have been found to move out of their homes, become professionals, become secondary or many times primary bread earners in a family. Initially women were found to be teachers, nurses, doctors etc but then with the advent of 1990s, they have been found to take up more challenging roles. They have been found to be more aspiring. Women have successfully proven themselves in several such spheres where the society had reservations. This country now has significant representation of women in the police force, in the army. The country has now even got its first group of fighter pilots. Women in this country today are mostly being found to juggle their domestic chores and professional commitments successfully and the wonderful thing is that in many cases, their male counterparts are extending a helping hand to them which is motivating and progressive in nature.

However when it comes to making a holistic comment of the status of women in today's India is concerned, we are unable to tell all things which are progressive since there still exists many houses in this country where women are leading claustrophobic lives, they are barred from making public appearances, barred from making their own choices about their lives, barred from eating what they like. There are houses where marital rapes happen every other night; where elders in the family physically assault minors rampantly and threat them with dire consequences if their open their mouth. While the country finds its pride at the Olympics being rescued by women athletes of this country, it still considers its women folk unworthy of being entrusted with bigger responsibilities. There have been many women achievers in this country across professional domains but then societal hurdles have prevented them from being not just inspirational but also play a role in making more women of this country come forward and take up active roles in public life.

Even in professional circuits we find women being paid less for the same job they are doing as their male counterparts. Take a look at the corporate boardrooms in this country, take a look at politics, a look at the sports circuit; everywhere there is gender discrimination. Women are being made to feel they are weaker, they are not at par, they are inferior and they are best suited for domestic chores and not fit to challenge men in any stream.

Depiction of Women in Indian Advertisements

India is a country where sex role is highly related to the prevailing religious and cultural backdrop. The complexion of a society and family are factors that also play a key role in the sex role development of individuals. As discussed earlier in this chapter women are by and large dominated by their male counterparts and there is an element of passive submission that is integrated in the traits of women in this country and strangely but factually it is irrespective of the level of education and professional expertise of a woman. Women by and large go by what the societal norms and expectations dictate.

Most Indian women of today still have faith in their age old customs and although they are portrayed as liberated, but at the same time, they are traditional in many aspects. Women of this country are taking up greater challenges in their professions and yet they have a keen sense of responsibility towards their household and children. This probably is a description of the modern Indian woman who is confident of maintaining healthy work-life balance.

With the kind of developments mentioned above, advertisers of today are often in a dilemma when it comes to portraying women. They are often puzzled to take a call on whether to depict them in traditional roles or in modern and liberated roles.

During the era of print only medium of advertising in this country, men were portrayed as bread winners, decision makers and professionals, whereas, women were portrayed as ones cooking meals, taking care of household activities or being concerned with their own appearance and that too to please and woo their love interests. Also when advertising in movies and on television happened in this country, motherhood and home-making were highlighted

as women's highest goal. Women were represented as those beings in the society who were meant to take care of their homes and their roles were limited to being housewives, dependent on men, with negligible purchasing capacity, and rarely as professionals. The 1970s, one of the most turbulent decades in this country witnessed women being depicted in advertisements as housewives, bandaging wounds or feeding their husbands and children, as sex objects, without any identity or as dependent where they need men to solve their problems.

During the 1980s, with greater access to education, and the germination of feminist movement in this country, the roles and expectations of women changed not only in the society but also in the way they were represented in advertisements. There were advertisements that depicted women who could think independently about various matters concerning them. Even as a housewife, they were shown to not just go to the market for shopping but negotiate well with sellers to get the best bargain for themselves and their family members.

Since the 1990s, women as independent, single, working individuals have been reported on Indian television. There have been advertisements that show how well a woman can take care of family during period of crisis in family like the demise of her husband. Advertisements for brands like Life Insurance Corporation (LIC) with the tagline "Zindagi ke Saath Bhi. Zindagi ke baad bhi" is one that can be cited over here where a widow is seen successfully marrying off her daughter and fulfilling the unfinished tasks of her husband by managing the finances post her husband's death.

The portrayal of women in Indian advertisements have come a long way today from being a docile housewife promoting household products and health and hygiene product to someone who is a more confident, liberated individual having the willingness and capacity to think on her own and take important decisions concerning one's life. Women in most advertisements today are shown as someone rooted to one's culture but at the same time not willing to accept life as it is; rather create something more exciting for herself. She is no more someone who is meant just to satiate the requirements of her household but is someone who believes in making a difference both to her home as well as in the outside world. Even when women today are depicted in advertisements that show her in home settings, she is seldom shown as someone who is a vulnerable and blunt individual; rather someone around whom the family sticks and supports and considers her the homemaker and not the traditional housewife. In other words, looking after the household and its requirements today is no longer depicted as a thankless job but something that the male members of a family should value and try

their level best to partner with the woman of the family in doing certain household chores.

As we switch on our televisions today, we are greeted by a plethora of brand advertisements and most of them do feature women in various avatars like a homemaker, a professional, a college student, a sister, a seductress and many more and trust me we get to see an evolved Indian woman on our television screens. There is a sprint in her body language, we find her male counterparts considering her an equal and not a being to be simply dominated. Women in Indian advertisements today are shown as carefree, reasonable, articulate, responsible, committed and tech savvy individuals who have the guts to take on the world and prove herself. In the contemporary era women have often been presented as achievers and as 'been there seen that' individuals and one big reason behind this change definitely is the way our societal structure and the perceptions and attitude towards women in society have evolved over the years.

PLOTS

This section of the book mentions some of the trendsetting advertisements registered in the Indian advertising annals. The advertisements are path breaking as far as portrayal of women in advertisements is concerned. There is something radical about the advertisements; radical in the way they have highlighted women and the world around them. Aspects like women's emancipation, gender equality, uninhibited display of emotion in public domain, women's economic empowerment, single and independent women have been exhibited through the various ads discussed. Many conventional thoughts, perceptions and attitudes towards women have been shattered in these advertisements and a positive paradigm shift towards women empowerment in the society has been noticed in these advertisements.

1.

'BATHING = EMANCIPATION'?
THE LIRIL EQUATION

Brand: Liril

Product: Bathing Soap

Year/Decade: 1974

Ad Agency: Lintas (now Lowe Lintas & Partners)

Can the act of bathing be a form of liberation? Can it be a form of escapism? Can it be a way to rejuvenating oneself and discovering a fresh persona in oneself? The answer to all these questions is an emphatic YES and this answer came for the first time in the history of Indian advertising through a brand called Liril-India's first lime based soap which was positioned as 'The Freshness Soap'.

The advertisement that was conceived sometime during the mid 1970s was so convincing, so impactful in its content that even today when you hear the tune "La, lalala, la, la, la" and you recall the brand name. Not just that, you even recall a pretty girl having fun under a waterfall bathing with a green bikini on. The colour green amplifying the freshness quotient attached with the soap. In fact there were various other elements too that amplified the freshness quotient – a fresh face to promote the brand first of all, the act of bathing which signifies the cleansing process, visuals of fresh lime slices from time to time within the advertisement, the background tune and the final voiceover which talks of discovering a 'fresh identity' of oneself by bathing with Liril.

The advertisement was conceived by one of the doyens of Indian advertising – Alyque Padamsee along with another colleague of his at Lintas, the advertising agency for the Hindustan Unilever  (then Hindustan Lever) Soap, Neena Merchant. The creative fodder came to Padamsee via a consumer survey that revealed that the Indian housewife, the target audience for the soap had time for herself only once during the day for about 15 minutes when she went for her bath. It was an act of escapism and liberation for her when she 'daydreamed'. It was the time when she wanted to forget her struggles as a housewife and simply enjoy her bath. This was to be seen in the advertisement too where visuals of the model Karen Lunel having fun under a waterfall were to be seen along with visuals of a woman bathing in her bathroom.

This advertisement was revolutionary in the history of Indian advertising since it was one of the first ads that really highlighted women's emancipation. The advertisement had no element of vulgarity; rather it was pure act of uninhibited fun being experienced by a woman. Here was a woman who enjoyed her own time in the way she liked throwing caution and conservatism to the winds. The advertisement definitely ensured to amplify the brand promise and the positioning statement because of which it has stood out to be one of the most durable women centric advertisements in Indian advertising annals.

2.

_____ KI KHARIDARI MEIN HI
SAMAJHDARI HAI

Brand: Surf

Product: Detergent Powder

Year/Decade: 1970s

Ad Agency: Lintas (now Lowe Lintas & Partners)

I am sure it took less than a second for you to fill in the blank space in the title. It is because the tagline is well etched in our memory for the way it was presented to us on Indian television and on various other media platforms several decades back.

This advertisement featuring a sparkling white saree clad character called 'Lalita ji' was so emphatic in driving home the brand promise that we recall this advertisement without much fuss even today. The ad germinated as a competitive strategy to counter the growing popularity of the cheaper washing powder viz. Nirma that was launched in 1969. This advertisement was another masterstroke executed by legendary adman Alyque Padamsee of Lintas.

There were several aspects of this commercial that has made this advertisement really memorable and something that i am compelled to cite when i speak of the 'empowered' woman in Indian advertising. Yes the 'empowered' woman who speaks her mind, who is no way a blunt persona and who knows how to bargain for articles in a bazaar to squeeze maximum savings out of her purchases. Lalita ji was the first on screen persona who went a long way in effectively erasing a common myth among we Indians that it makes sense to buy cheap products whereas the fact is there is a huge difference between buying a 'sasti cheez' and  buying a 'achchi cheez'. This was the ad that halted the growing popularity of Nirma by serving as an eye opener for many to value the virtues of a product that was a bit expensive but then it was worth the penny being paid since 1 kg of a 'sasti washing powder' was equivalent to just '½ kg of Surf' functionally. All these messages were made loud and clear by a woman who had a strong and empowered persona named Lalita ji. We talk of

'SHERO' genre of movies and this advertisement of Surf was the first women centric advertisement that can well be claimed as one belonging to the aforesaid genre.

3.

THE TASTE OF ECONOMIC EMPOWERMENT

Brand: Amul

Product: Dairy Product

Year/Decade: 1990s

Ad Agency: FCB Ulka

Economic empowerment is always a cherished premise especially if that is concerned with rural women. Since Independence, this country has witnessed most of its rural populace living in abject poverty but then it took a genius like Dr Verghese Kurien to usher 'White Revolution' in this country through his 'Operation Flood project' which was all about enhancing the supply of milk in this country and ensuring that the farmers got the deserved sum of money for the milk and other dairy products they supplied.

Coming to the brand communication of Amul, a brand owned by Gujarat Cooperative Milk Marketing Federation (GCMMF) has been in the limelight since the 1960s with its weekly hoardings (in the form of cartoon strips) that featured the Amul girl mimicking certain important events across domains happening within and outside the country.

Manthan was a Hindi movie directed by Shyam Benegal starring Girish Karnad and Smita Patil that was released in 1976 to commemorate the 'White Revolution' in this country. It featured how the cooperative movement revolving around milk transformed a certain part of this country named Anand in the state of Gujarat economy

wise. It also featured how this movement lifted the economic status of  women in the society who were actively involved in bringing milk to the nearest milk processing plants from where it got supplied across the length and breadth of this country.

Some 20 years after the release of this movie, we got to see the Amul Manthan advertisement on our TV screens. There was a prime time program on Doordarshan those days named Amul Surabhi that was anchored by Siddharth Kak and Renuka Sahane and it was during that program, we used to see this advertisement which had 50% of the visuals taken from the movie Manthan. Rest of the visuals were related to the logistics and supply chain process involved. It also featured how this cooperative movement transformed the state of living of the villagers and its women and their children. The advertisement reflects happy faces of mothers and their children. The climax of this advertisement emphatically

 summarized the transformation process heralded by the cooperative movement initiated by Dr Kurien as it mentioned some extremely encouraging statistics. "Every morning 27 lac women across 13,000 villages, bringing in milk worth Rs 20 crores, are now celebrating their economic independence thanks to the co-operative movement called Amul." The commercial has a song with the flavour of rural Gujarat playing in the background which was sung by Priti Sagar that really

enhanced the overall experience of watching and appreciating the advertisement. The lyrics of the song clearly mention the generous production and supply of milk and its corresponding effect in terms of economic betterment (doodh ka sagar behta jaaye, kangan sone ki khankaye) and also about the major outcome of the cooperative movement viz, the advent of Goddess Lakshmi in various rural households. The advertisement signs off with the tagline – "The Taste of India".

If we take a look at the contemporary times at some of the advertisements of Amul Milk with the tagline "Amul Doodh peeta hai India", we find that there are some really well conceived ads that talk about raising a toast to women power. It celebrates the grit, power and determination of women and highlight the fact that women can surely be achievers across professional verticals.

4.

THE SWAAD OF LIFE. THE SWAAD OF CADBURY DAIRY MILK

Brand: Cadbury Dairy Milk

Product: Chocolate

Year/Decade: 1990s

Ad Agency: Ogilvy & Mather (O&M)

The girl is biting into a bar of Cadbury Dairy Milk. There is a cricket match going on. The scoreboard reads 99. A delivery is bowled and the batsman hits a shot in the air. There is a man who straight away puts his hand on his forehead to signify a 'lost case'. There is a fielder who is attempting to get under the ball to catch it. The girl is found praying to God that no unfortunate thing happens and may the ball sail above the boundary ropes and so does it and then? And then what happens happened for the first time in Indian advertising history as we find the girl hugging her friends, dodges the policeman who tries to stop her from entering the field and then she breaks into an uninhibited and impromptu jig. The batsman in question (clearly portrayed as the girl's love interest) is embarrassed to see the girl's impromptu reaction as he hides his face with his gloves on. The final scene of the advertisement shows the two sharing a bar of Cadbury Dairy Milk as the tagline appears 'The Real Taste of Life" and the voiceover says "Cadbury Dairy Milk Asli Swaad Zindagi Ka".

Traditionally women in this country have always been asked to stay reserved especially in the public domain. They are supposed to be calm, quiet and not display any sort of unwarranted

or unexpected conduct and here was this advertisement

that heralded the emergence of the new generation women in this country who were uninhibited and who had no issues about expressing their true feelings and actions in the public domain. The advertisement features a liberated woman who had no qualms about throwing caution to the winds and sharing a private moment with her love interest in full public view. The above mentioned aspects of the advertisement clearly makes this commercial a trendsetter of sorts when it comes of portrayal of women in Indian advertising.

This advertisement was conceived by acclaimed adman Piyush Pandey to reposition the brand when chocolates as a product category were perceived to be only meant for children. The advertisement ensured the enhanced and broadened consumption of the product across new consumer segments. Cadbury Dairy Milk was re positioned as a brand that was absolutely okay to be consumed across age brackets to celebrate life and its moments.

5.

FROM 'HOUSEWIFE' TO 'HOMEMAKER'

Brand: Whirlpool

Product: Home Appliances

Year/Decade: 1990s

Ad Agency: FCB Ulka

If there is one advertisement of a brand that truly made we Indians wake up, recognize, appreciate and respect the activities of the Indian housewife, it's got to be the advertisement for Whirlpool home appliances that was beamed on Indian television sometime in the late 1990s. Before this occurrence, it was not just we men folk who used to think that looking after the home was a worthless and insignificant activity but even women who were not employed felt and often expressed publicly that they were an insignificant lot since they were not contributing to family income and were dependent on their husbands financially. Looking after the home and performing the daily chores was considered too easy an activity and unworthy of being glorified in any way.

However the Whirlpool advertisement highlighting the 6th Sense technology of the brand became a trendsetter as it described the job of looking after the home in a more respectable and glorified manner by coining the word – 'homemaker'. This word was instantly acceptable to not just those women folk who were housewives as they felt more dignified in describing themselves as homemakers rather than housewives but also their children and their husbands too felt better while describing the fulcrum persona of their house as engaged in homemaking. The word 'homemaker' was used to describe all such women

who were managers of the house, active catalysts, who were in control of all household affairs and were a source of emotional support as well.

Speaking of the advertisement, it featured a new age woman actively controlling the house as a tech savvy individual as she operates the microwave, AC, refrigerator and washing machine with élan. Her husband and children are just amazed to see her efficiency and the immaculate way she is looking after the various aspects of her house. The ad ends with the tagline – "You and Whirlpool. The world's best Homemakers". This advertisement thus just did not add a personality facet to the brand and made it more lively and acceptable to its target audiences but also got itself registered in Indian advertising history as one such advertisement that redefined the idea and dignity of being a woman who dedicates all her life for the well being of her home and nothing else.

6.

Betiyaan bhi khaas hoti hain

Brand: HDFC Standard Life (now HDFC Life)

Product: Insurance

Year/Decade: 2008

Ad Agency: Leo Burnett

Betiyaan or daughters in this country have traditionally been thought of as 'paraya dhan' or meant for someone else. She is to be brought up somehow by the parents with all the right 'sanskars' so that once she attains the marriageable age, she can be married off without much hassle (read dowry etc). Parents have shirked to make investments related to education on the girl child. They have shunned the idea of daughters earning before marriage since they can no way take her earnings for consumption in case such a need arises. Daughters are so 'distant' to their parents that traditional norms in this country say that once a daughter gets married, her parents do not even consume the water of her 'in laws'' place.

I recall distinctly two advertisements created by Leo Burnett advertising agency for its client HDFC Standard Life (now HDFC Life) that compelled many parents in this country to rethink what they feel about their daughters and their capabilities.

Let's consider this advertisement where an aged father is  seen trying to mend his old 'small' car. The daughter is seen signing a cheque while she asks her father that isn't it time for him to consider purchasing a new car and that too a big one. The father asks the reason for buying a big car to which the daughter says that she wants her father to travel in style in a big car. The father laughs as he asks "Extra paise tera dad dega kya" to which his daughter says, "Nahi extra paise degi mere dad ki beti" as she handovers the cheque to her father. The father has an initial hesitation in accepting the cheque but then daughter successfully persuades her father. The mother joins at this juncture and enquires about the matter to which the father says "Car badi ho gayi aur beti bhi". The ad signs off with the tagline "Sar Utha Ke Jiyo".

Another advertisement that i can recall in bits and pieces is the one for a children's policy from the HDFC stable. Over here we see a young girl going through a book on space objects and expresses her wish to be a space  scientist when she grows up. She is quick to think that she will require a rocket to reach space and for that thing to happen lot of money will be required. After discussing on the possibility of her maternal uncle financing her dream, the father says that there is a better option which is by the time she grows up to realize her dream, her father will accumulate enough money to finance her dream to which the young girl happily agrees to. So see over here another traditional custom/norm is kicked off that parents should abstain from making investments on their girl child. The concept of gender equality, equal opportunity and equal recognition has been well brought out through these advertisements with the tagline – "Sar Utha ke Jiyo". The advertisements aim at greater common good than just garnering eyeballs and subsequent conversions for the insurance brand.

7.

Marriages are made on dot coms!

Brands: Jeevansathi.com & Bharatmatrimony.com

Product: Online Matrimonial Portals

Years: 2011 & 2013

Ad Agencies: FCB Ulka & Lowe Lintas & Partners

For decades, arranged marriages in this country have happened through classified advertisements in leading national and regional dailies. The family of the prospective bride or the groom were found to advertise in the newspaper regarding the kind of match they were looking for their daughter or son. In response to which they used to receive letters and calls from various households and then further talks were held with suitable parties. Thus matchmaking has been happening for several years through newspapers. However with onset of the Internet revolution in this country and proliferation of various types of portals in the online space, portals dedicated to online matchmaking came into existence. Since there was a growing trend among the wannabe grooms and brides to be more vocal about what they wanted from their prospective life partners and since this online space was something they were savvier about, they took control of initiating matchmaking through the online portals. Mostly it were the boys and girls who uploaded their profile and then mentioned about the kind of life partner they were looking for. Prospective brides and grooms or their family members used to come across suitable profiles and then they would initiate contact with the kind of resources they had at their disposal. The portals offered both free and paid registrations and obviously there were certain tangible advantages attached with the later. Some of the prominent online portals in the matrimonial space over the years have been bharatmatrimony.com, shaadi.com and jeevansathi.com.

In 2011, Jeevansathi.com cashing on the trend of allowing prospective brides and grooms to take the major decision of choosing their life partners with parents offering background support in terms of sharing their opinions and advice came up with an entertaining advertisement. Here was a girl whose father was scouting for a suitable son-in-law. Wherever the girl went with her father and interacted with any boy or wherever the father found a boy interesting enough to be his future son-in-law he was found to gather his daughter's views on the person by attempting to place the 'sehra' (worn by grooms during marriage) on the head of that boy. The situations presented were extremely humorousand the girl clearly expressed that she did not like her father's crazy deeds to scout for a son-in-law. At this juncture, the voiceover says, "Aur bhi

hai raaste jeevansathi pane ke.." The girl was found logging on to the jeevansathi.com site and check the profile of a prospective groom. Her expressions suggested that she liked the profile and the father once again attempts to place the 'sehra' on the picture of the boy to be seen on the computer screen. The girl was found to nod her head to this suggesting that she was interested to marry the boy. The advertisement ends with the tagline "We match better".

The advertisement clearly highlighted the fact that this country was changing for the good when it came to arranged marriages in this country. Instead of parents taking the whole and sole decision regarding who will be the best match for their wards, the prospective grooms and brides were given the opportunity to take the most crucial decision of their lives backed by the support, advice and opinions of parents. The advertisement was special since it highlighted a major paradigm shift in parent's attitudes towards their daughters and giving them the freedom to choose their life partners.

In 2013, bharatmatrimony.com came up with an advertisement created by Lowe Lintas & Partners that i consider was another milestone in portraying the enhanced recognition and respect that women in this country were getting in the contemporary society. The advertisement showed the husband having dinner with his parents. The wife was absent at the dining table. The husband is asked by her mother if he regularly has his meal before his wife arrives from her workplace to which her son says no normally they are used to having dinner together and perhaps she might have got stuck due to some reason at her workplace and hence she was late on that day. The father is found asking that when after his son's promotion, the expenses of the house can be easily taken care of what is the need for his wife to work? The wife is found meanwhile making an entry in home and standing just outside the dining room and overhearing the conversations. She found her husband responding to his father's

question by stating that she works not to run the home but she works because she likes to work. The wife is found to recall at this juncture that she mentioned on the bharatmatrimony.com portal while uploading her profile that she will like to work even after marriage. The wife is pleased to find that her husband has accommodated and respected her wish and she makes a smiling entry into the dining room to have her dinner with the family. The voiceover says "Hum unse milate hain jo aapko samjh paate hain". The advertisement signs off with the tagline "for happy marriages".

The advertisement of bharatmatrimony.com thus once again shows how society and its outlook towards women are surely changing in the right direction. The advertisements for the online portals mentioned above were clearly trendsetters in highlighting some of the major and positive paradigm shifts happening as far as perceptions and attitudes towards women are concerned.

8.

IT'S ALL ABOUT FEELING BEAUTIFUL

Brand: Dove

Product: Soap

Year/Decade: 2014

Ad Agency: Ogilvy & Mather (O&M)

The advertisement starts with the following female voiceover, "Isn't it strange that in a country of 631 million women, there is still only one face of beauty when there is so much more to be admired." The ad first zooms on one pretty face and then a myriad faces of women start getting featured in succession. The ad features women of all complexions, all sizes, all ages, all outfits and all professions. Finally the ad ends with the tagline "Let's break the rules of beauty". The ad is of Dove.

The brand, a product from the Hindustan Unilever stable has always been found to adopt a radically different and rational approach to advertising since its launch in India. In the initial days of the brand, we got to see the litmus paper test being conducted to highlight its moisturizing capacity and its benefit on skin. However sometime after 2010, the brand has been found to do away with certain myths related to beauty in women. It has been successful in sending out strong messages to women the world over about feeling beautiful the way they are and not go for beauty treatments etc that often have detrimental effects.

 Coming back to this advertisement that was conceived sometime in 2016 and the video for the advertisement was made by award winning documentary maker Pan Nalin. The beauty of the advertisement was that none of the faces featured in the advertisement were professional models but then all of them contributed to making the ad look and feel special. The advertisement sends out a clear message to women that do not get judged about your beauty by others. Rather you should feel beautiful the way you are. Beautiful should be a woman's persona, her conduct and the way she carries herself and the confidence within her more than anything else. There is no point in being physically attractive but blunt. The

tagline for the advertisement summarizes the entire concept in one short, effective and durable sentence.

9.

..AND WOMEN ARE SELF SUSTAINABLE

Brand: Titan Raga

Product: Watch

Year: 2014

Ad Agency: Ogilvy & Mather (O&M)

The advertisement i am going to mention now is categorized as celebrity endorsement in the marketing lexicon. They are basically those advertisements where a brand is promoted by a celebrity (a personality from the field of cinema, sports etc who is well known in the public domain). The success of such advertisements has a lot to do with the selection of a celebrity for endorsing a brand and the match or gel happening between the celebrity and the brand being endorsed. In this particular advertisement, all the above mentioned parameters are well met.

The brand in question is Titan Raga and the celebrity is actress Nimrat Kaur who has delivered convincing performances in movies like Lunchbox and Airlift. The advertisement opens with Kaur reading a book at the airport lounge when she suddenly gets to meet her former boyfriend. When she enquires how is he doing, the man says that he is just the way he was when she left her. The man finds out that Kaur is still not married post which he says that things could have worked between them if she only agreed not to work post marriage. This makes Kaur look at her Titan Raga watch, run her fingers around it and say that her former boyfriend was right in describing how he is presently because he is still

just the way he was when she left her. The ad signs off with the female voiceover stating "Khud se naya rishta" and the brand is mentioned after that.

Internationally De Beers was extremely successful when they launched the 'Right Hand Ring" campaign for its diamonds with focus on independent women and to me this advertisement is the Indian version of a similar thought being executed. While speaking about this advertisement, Piyush Pandey, executive Chairman and creative director, O&M, South Asia mentioned that Raga is an 'evolved' watch for the 'evolved' woman of today who is self respecting and confident. The ad film was directed by Vivek Kakkad of Curious Films, an ad production house.

Women do not require any financial/emotional support to sustain in life. Just like men, if they are skilled enough, they can find their own way out to sustain independently in this world and not compromise on their opinions, beliefs, dreams and wishes. They need to have faith in themselves, love themselves and should forge a strong relationship with themselves if they do not find someone in their lives who will allow them to lead life on their own terms and allow them the space they require. All the above aspects have been well highlighted in the advertisement in a convincing manner through the advertisement's plot and content.

***

ABOUT THE AUTHOR

Dr. Kisholoy Roy is a PhD in Management from IIT (Indian School of Mines), Dhanbad. He is a certified Accredited Management Teacher (AMT) who has been into teaching Management for several years now at the post graduate level. Dr Roy has authored several books on management apart from authoring various case studies, articles and research papers. He is presently engaged as an independent trainer and consultant in digital marketing and brand communication apart from his engagements as a faculty in Marketing with various B-schools.